LIFE

America's Most Scenic Drives

On the Nation's Highways and Byways

LIFE

Editor Robert Sullivan
Creative Director Ian Denning
Picture Editor Barbara Baker Burrows
Executive Editor Robert Andreas
Art Director Rick DeMonico
Associate Picture Editor Christina Lieberman
Writer-Reporters Hildegard Anderson (Chief),
Carol Vinzant
Copy JC Choi (Chief), Mimi McGrath, Wendy Williams
Production Manager Michael Roseman
Picture Research Rachel Hendrick
Photo Assistant Joshua Colow
Consulting Picture Editors
Suzanne Hodgart (London), Tala Skari (Paris)

Publisher Andrew Blau
Finance Director Craig Ettinger
Assistant Finance Manager Karen Tortora

Editorial Operations Richard K. Prue (Director),
Richard Shaffer (Manager), Brian Fellows, Raphael Joa,
Stanley E. Moyse (Supervisors), Keith Aurelio, Gregg Baker,
Charlotte Coco, Scott Dvorin, Kevin Hart, Rosalie Khan,
Po Fung Ng, Barry Pribula, David Spatz, Vaune Trachtman,
Sara Wasilausky, David Weiner

Time Inc. Home Entertainment

President Rob Gursha
Vice President, Branded Businesses David Arfine
Vice President, New Product Development Richard Fraiman
Executive Director, Marketing Services Carol Pittard
Director, Retail & Special Sales Tom Mifsud
Director of Finance Tricia Griffin
Assistant Marketing Director Ann Marie Doherty
Prepress Manager Emily Rabin
Book Production Manager Jonathan Polsky
Associate Product Manager Jennifer Dowell

Special thanks to Bozena Bannett, Alex Bliss, Bernadette
Corbie, Robert Dente, Gina Di Meglio, Anne-Michelle Gallero,
Peter Harper, Suzanne Janso, Robert Marasco, Natalie McCrea,
Mary Jane Rigoroso, Steven Sandonato, Grace Sullivan

Published by

LIFE Books

"LIFE" is a trademark of
Time Inc.

Time Inc.
271 Avenue of the Americas,
New York, NY 10020

ISBN: 1-932273-21-2
Library of Congress Control
Number: 2004090499

We welcome your comments
and suggestions about LIFE
Books. Please write to us at:
LIFE Books, Attention:
Book Editors, PO Box 11016,
Des Moines, IA 50336-1016

If you would like to order any
of our hardcover Collector's
Edition books, please call us
at 1-800-327-6388 (Monday
through Friday, 7:00 a.m.–
8:00 p.m. or Saturday, 7:00
a.m.–6:00 p.m. Central Time).

Please visit us, and sample
past editions of LIFE, at
www.LIFE.com.

Iconic images from the LIFE Picture Collection are now available
as fine art prints and posters. The prints are reproductions
on archival, resin-coated photographic paper, framed in black
wood, with an acid-free mat. Works by the famous LIFE
photographers—Eisenstaedt, Parks, Bourke-White, Burrows,
among many others—are available. The LIFE poster collection
presents large-format, affordable, suitable-for-framing
images. For more information on the prints, priced at $99 each,
call 888-933-8873 or go to www.purchaseprints.com. The
posters may be viewed and ordered at www.LIFEposters.com.

Sweet Bay Pond, Everglades National Park, Fla.
Previous pages: the Hawaiian island of Maui;
Bixby Bridge, Big Sur, Calif.

Tim Fitzharris

The American Top 40

So . . . where to go?

It all depends on whom you ask. If you ask the folks at the United States Forest Service, they will tell you to head for one of the 136 official National Forest Scenic Byways. If you try the U.S. Bureau of Land Management, they will hand you their list of 58 Back Country Byways—also official, of course. If you inquire of the National Park Service, you will learn of the four

If you ask the Society of American Travel Writers, they'll give you a Top 10, and if you ask *Travel+Leisure* magazine, they'll be happy to give you an opinion. If you ask Fred and Ethel next door, they'll tell you that, sure, the Kancamagus is nice, but if you go down High Country Lane and hang a right onto Maple and then a left onto the dirt road—keep your eyes open, there's no sign—then follow that down to Peaceful Pond and drive

Stephen Wilkes (2)

Coast-to-coast splendor, from Maine . . .

National Parkways. If you query the Federal Highway Administration, they will point you toward 96 America's Byways, 75 of which are National Scenic Byways and 21 of which get the added designation All-American Roads, which means, in the eyes of the judges, that they are superior among equals. Even with overlap—some Scenic Byways are in National Parks or National Forests and appear on multiple lists—that adds up to more than 250 scenic highways and byways in the U.S.A.

round in there while the foliage is flaming, why, there's no more beautiful road in the world.

The thing is, they're all right. They are all absolutely correct.

But you're asking us. So, LIFE went to all of the above-mentioned folks and ladled in their nominations, whisked in our own, then did some distilling. First, we came up with our Hall of Famers: No volume about the most scenic drives in America would be worth its Death Valley salt marsh without California's Route 1, or Going-to-the-Sun

Road in Montana, or the extraordinary stretch over the Florida Keys, or the north-south meander through Vermont known as "One Hundred," or any of the others in the must-see-in-your-lifetime category. Then we cross-referenced the sanctioned designees of the anointing agencies. Then we caucused among ourselves and made personal pitches for roads that we knew to be spectacular. Then we asked our country-trotting photographers if they had strong feelings about the most beautiful road they had seen and shot. Finally we flipped a coin, and kicked out Nos. 41 and 42 and 43, because a Top 40 seemed like a nice collection, one that an auto-tourist might use as a life list.

Legendary Route 66 is explained, as are the Post Road, the Lincoln Highway, even the Las Vegas Strip. However, we cannot recommend these to you, gentle reader, as among America's most scenic drives. If they once existed as such, they no longer do. (Or, as with Vegas, their "scenic-ness" is of a distinctly unnatural kind.) Some of them are, now, little more than roads of the mind; if you follow Route 1 from Maine to Florida, you risk more than road rage, you are inviting insanity. Route 1's glory days are squarely in the rearview mirror.

In this volume's pictures and accompanying text, we hope to convey a feeling for the road in

. . . to California

As a rule, the mileages that we discuss in describing each roadway define the sections that we consider optimal for driving and viewing pleasure. Most of these thoroughfares are open year-round, some are seasonal. Because we have a respect for history, we mention it where pertinent. Speaking of which: Placed between the various regions as we traipse across the country—regions that follow guidelines established by the Highway Administration's Byways program—are short features about some of America's most storied roads.

question, and the rewards that await. In the pages immediately following this introduction, there is information on how to obtain the details you might want about these drives. Our intention here is not to be a Fodor's guide, noble enterprise though it is. We are LIFE, and what we do is seek to inspire or entice or excite through photography. We hope that this book is, then, an inspiration, an enticement, a spur to the excitement that awaits on the open road.

You got the keys? Let's go.

The Top 40

LIFE has researched each of these drives, and suggests the following Web sites and contact numbers. Also, three of the federal agencies in the scenic-road-designating business offer help on the Web and by phone. Useful material on the Federal Highway Administration's 75 National Scenic Byways, including free packets of info and maps, may be ordered at www.byways.org, or by calling (800) 429-9297. The Forest Service sells maps at www.fs.fed.us, and can be reached at (202) 205-8333. The National Park Service can be contacted at www.nps.gov, and (202) 208-6843. A fine clearinghouse for information on traveling scenic routes across the United States is available at www.recreation.gov, in the "auto touring" section.

13 Red River Gorge Scenic Byway, Ky.
606-677-6096
www.kyappalachians.com/
scenic_byways.htm

14 Shawnee National Forest Drive, Ill.
800-248-4373
www.southernmostillinois.com

4 The Merritt Parkway, Conn.
203-661-3255
www.merrittparkway.com

5 Skyline Drive, Va.
540-999-3500
www.nps.gov/shen

15 Covered Bridge Scenic Byway, Ohio
740-373-9055
www.fs.fed.us/r9/wayne

6 The Blue Ridge Parkway, N.C. and Va.
828-298-0398
www.nps.gov/blri

16 The Amish Road, Ind.
800-262-8161
www.amishcountry.org

7 Cherokee Foothills Scenic Highway, S.C.
800-849-4766
www.theupcountry.com

17 Route 22, Mich.
800-442-2084
www.wmta.org

1 The Acadia Loop, Maine
207-288-3338
www.acadia.national-park.com

8 Sea Islands, Ga.
800-847-4842
www.gacoast.com

18 North Shore Scenic Drive, Minn.
800-438-5884
www.visitduluth.com

2 The Kancamagus Highway, N.H.
800-346-3687
www.visitwhitemountains.com

9 Route 9336, Fla.
305-242-7700
www.nps.gov/ever

19 Edge of the Wilderness Scenic Byway, Minn.
888-868-7476
www.exploreminnesota.com

3 Route 100, Vt.
800-837-6668
www.1-800-vermont.com

10 The Overseas Highway, Fla.
800-352-5397
www.fla-keys.com

20 Peter Norbeck and Custer Scenic Byways, S.D.
605-773-3301
www.travelsd.com

11 Natchez Trace Parkway, Ala., Miss., Tenn.
800-305-7417
www.nps.gov/natr

21 North Unit Scenic Drive, N.D.
701-842-2333
www.ndtourism.com

12 Old Spanish Trail, La.
800-346-1958
www.lafayettetravel.com

22 Arkansas Scenic 7 Byway, Ark.
501-682-7777
www.arkansas.com

39

40

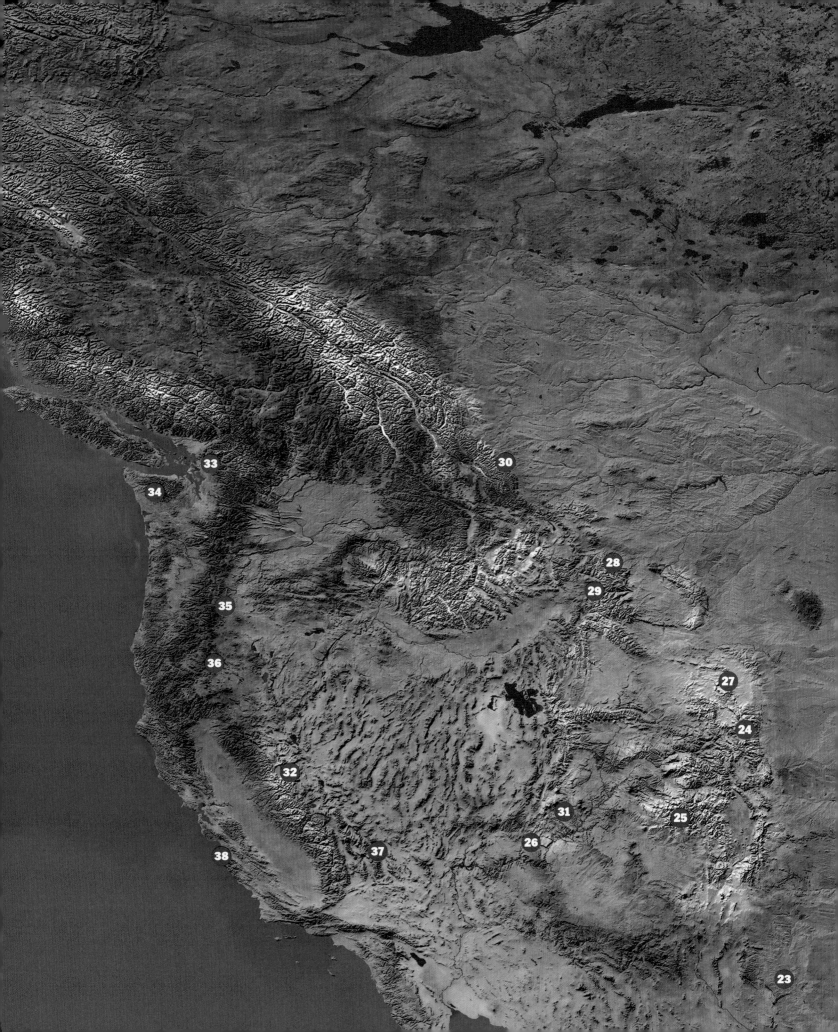

A winter field, near Route 100 in Vermont

From Maine to Virginia

The Acadia Loop

Maine

Every mile of the long road that hugs the often rugged Maine coast has an attraction: the original L.L. Bean outpost in Freeport; a dozen acres of outlet stores right nearby; a rustic shack with picnic benches adjacent in the grove, where you can avail yourself of the best lobster roll you've ever eaten. In Ogunquit and Kennebunk are the beaches, in Boothbay and Bar Harbor the surf is splashing over rocks, and farther north—US 1 from Ellsworth to Calais and beyond—the undeveloped coast and high ocean conjure Cornwall, Cypress Point and Vikings. The crown jewel of the Maine coast is Cadillac Mountain, located on Mount Desert Island in Acadia National Park (which includes Bar Harbor). Hang a right off US 1 to get to the 20-mile Park Loop Road, add the seven-mile up-and-back to the mountaintop—and you are authentically Down East.

Acadia's Thunder Hole

Fog at Little Hunter's Beach

On a park lake, a cormorant

In Acadia National Park, a blueberry and spruce bog

The Kancamagus Highway

New Hampshire

Legendary New Hampshire Governor Sherm Adams was wont to celebrate "the land above the notches" for its grandeur and uncompromising beauty. These White Mountains canyons—Pinkham Notch, Franconia Notch, Crawford Notch—are rough-hewn and impressive, with high, granitic slopes upthrust on either side of a valley roadway that is sublime to negotiate in summer, though often impossible in a midwinter storm. In fall foliage season, the canyons are a riot of color, but interestingly, it is a highway just below the notches that is considered the Holy Grail by leaf-peepers. The Kancamagus Highway, a.k.a. Route 112, from Lincoln east to Conway, which is paralleled for much of its length by the aptly named Swift River, is a 34-mile trip that begins as softly as a sonnet, rises to a middle act as dramatic as *The Tempest* and then descends to a denouement that is gentle and thoroughly rewarding.

Albany Bridge, built in 1858

Autumn light at Kancamagus Pass

Swift River near Rocky Gorge

Sugar maple saplings

Route 100
Vermont

Everyone from cow artist Woody Jackson to cheesemaker Cabot to ice cream kings Ben & Jerry to rock stars Phish to the boutique maple sugar harvester next door has traded on the earnest, honest, bucolic image that is Vermont. The fact is, the image is not a lie. All one has to do is hit the road anywhere along the nearly 200-mile Route 100 between Newport and Wilmington to have this confirmed. Travel a half hour and you'll hit a Vermont village or two: the mountain town of Stowe, where Von Trapp family harmonies drift through the icy air; homespun Waitsfield, where the locals ski Mad River Glen and dare you to join them; Stockbridge; Pittsfield; Weston; East Jamaica. Tin Pan Alley tunesmiths John Blackburn and Karl Suessdorf wrote a lyric that precisely captures this road through the heart of the Green Mountain State:

> *Evening summer breeze*
> *Warbling of a meadowlark*
> *Moonlight in Vermont*
> *You and I and Moonlight in Vermont*

The village of Stowe

Grazing sheep in Moretown, during early autumn

Michael Melford

Susan Lapides (2)

A Pittsfield barn; a Killington treescape

Michael Melford (2)

The Merritt Parkway
Connecticut

Those in a hurry choose to boom along multilane Interstate 95 in southern Connecticut, sometimes glimpsing Long Island Sound, sometimes too focused to even bother. Others take the northern route, 84, through decidedly unscenic Danbury and Waterbury. But the poets always opt for the Merritt, one of the country's first purposeful highways and one of the last remaining that combines the delights of a formal garden with a utilitarian purpose. Yes, a mosey through the Litchfield Hills in the northwest corner of this state is more . . . New Englandy. But the Merritt, which is on the route from New York City to Hartford, remains a singular experience. It twists and turns (those who exceed the 55-mph limit just don't get it, and should opt for I-95), and passes beneath stone-arched bridges that are the highway equivalent of Madison County. Built in the 1930s and 37.5 miles long, the Merritt—one of the few American roads listed on the National Register of Historic Places—is a classic, and ever will be.

Art deco wings on a Merritt overpass in Stratford

Only miles from Manhattan, Mother Nature

Lynda Richardson/Corbis

Galen Rowell/Mountain Light

The hills ablaze with color

Skyline Drive
Virginia

Just over a hundred miles in length, the highway from Front Royal south to Rockfish Gap is the ne plus ultra of a species of mid-Atlantic ridge-running roadway that offers the driver frequent and stunning views of and from the Blue Ridge Mountains. Spreading out splendidly to the west is the Shenandoah Valley with its eponymous river, while the foothills falling eastward are equally captivating. Were one driving foolishly, one could execute this trip in three hours. But with caverns to visit and so many overlooks to enjoy, each of them affording a more soul-stirring experience than the last, why be foolish? The recommended driving time here is five hours.

A northern harrier over Big Meadows

Raymond Gehman/Corbis

Sunrise over Shenandoah National Park

Galen Rowell/Mountain Light

Carr Clifton/Minden Pictures

Dogwood blossoms near Thornton Gap; white-tailed deer

The Blue Ridge Parkway

Virginia and North Carolina

This road, linking Shenandoah and Great Smoky Mountains national parks, a car path that is so rich and so enriching, was actually born in poverty, a classic example of the "make work" endeavors of the Great Depression. Initial funding came through the Public Works Administration, and laborers were also siphoned from the Work Projects Administration and the Civilian Conservation Corps. Private contractors were there too, providing much of the heavy construction. Some reports have it that the entire undertaking was really begun to provide jobs for idled mountaineers. In any case, the country is clearly the better for it. The Blue Ridge Parkway is 469 miles of pure Americana, paralleling the Appalachian Trail in its northern reaches and passing through Pisgah National Forest in its southern. The James River, Roanoke Mountain, Linville Falls: None are the longest, biggest or tallest, but they are perfect in and of themselves. And, thanks to "make work," they are today reachable by all.

Rolling toward Blue Ridge Overlook

Above, horses and
chestnut rail fences;
left, fog on Thunder
Ridge; opposite,
Mabry Mill

Underwood Archives

Route 1—The Post Road

The first postrider between New York and Boston set off in 1673 on old Indian trails; the trip took him two weeks. A century later, Revolutionary War soldiers tramped the same path along the belly of New England. Independence gained, the Boston Post Road became the country's first major thoroughfare—America's first interstate highway. In the 1800s, stagecoaches bragged of speeds averaging six miles per hour on a route linking 14 states, from Maine to Florida. When the federal highway system was launched in 1926, it was only fitting that this storied East Coast passage should become U.S. Route 1. The automobile brought a new vibrancy to what was now, in some places, affectionately called the Old Post Road. Hundreds of Howard Johnson's restaurants and mom-and-pop diners, a tribe of colossal Indian statues and other assorted kitsch—Stonehenge replicas in both New Hampshire and Georgia—were erected to beguile tourists into spending time and money. But after I-95 was rolled out on a parallel path in the '60s and '70s, everything changed. Route 1 became the afterthought passageway that could be cut apart, corseted or otherwise constrained by stop signs and traffic lights. Today, the Federal Highway Administration's unofficial historian, Richard F. Weingroff, says that Route 1 is about the ugliest and most inefficient of all U.S. highways. Of its 2,377 miles, only a dozen or so are designated as scenic—a final, very small tribute to the country's first great drive.

Clockwise from right: In 1937, the stretch between Washington, D.C., and Baltimore is still rather quaint; 18 years later, things are starting to heat up along that same route; down in Florida, the signs are clearly emerging triumphant; an earlier, quieter Florida, in Palm Beach, though there are already a lot of parked cars; tourist time in Maine.

Spanish moss on an oak in St. Martinville, La., along the Old Spanish Trail

Into the South

Cherokee Foothills Scenic Highway

South Carolina

The foothills in question are those of the Blue Ridge Mountains—or, as the Cherokees of yore called them, the Great Blue Hills of God. The drive runs roughly 130 miles along the border between the Carolinas before turning south and passing near Sumter National Forest. Along the way are serene meadows, high-country vistas of mountainous horizons, dense woodlands, glittering waterfalls and, finally, Hartwell Lake. As with other establishments and institutions in the region—a town, a county, a highway—the lake is named for one Nancy Hart, a strapping woman who, legend has it, dispatched one Tory, wounded another and helped capture still more at her house during the Revolutionary War. An enterprise of such vigor, combined with the fierce hostility visited upon the native Cherokees by subsequent generations of white settlers, seems wholly at odds with the peaceful, nourishing calm that pervades the Scenic Highway today.

Tom Blagden/Larry Ulrich Stock (2)

Slicking Falls at Table Rock Reservoir; Table Rock Mountain from Caesar's Head

Redbud at Station Cove Falls, Blue Ridge Escarpment

Twin Falls, Blue Ridge Escarpment

Macduff Everton/Corbis

Sea Islands

Georgia

Let's say you were going to drive from storied Jekyll Island, where Rockefellers lunched with Vanderbilts in the Gilded Age, up to that Athens of the antebellum South, Savannah. You could hop over to Interstate 95 and make the trip in less than two hours. Or you could meander 81 miles north on 17, with a little detour through the town of Meridian on 99, and thereby bathe yourself in the lush, rich atmosphere of the Georgian Gold Coast. The collection of barely offshore islands that includes Jekyll, St. Simons, Little St. Simons and Sea Island is known locally as the Golden Isles—a very discerning appellation. No less alluring are the estuaries and marshlands (the salt grasses in the Marshes of Glynn are mesmerizing) and the miles of pine forest that exist gently inland. The journey is the automotive equivalent of relaxing in the hammock on a warm midsummer's day.

Boardwalk at Jekyll Island

Shore birds above tide flats; opposite, two
aspects of Sea Island—massive live oaks,
and serene reed beds surrounding a stream

Route 9336
Florida

This is a 50-mile road through a river—the fantastic "River of Grass" that is the Everglades, a subtropical ecosystem unique on the planet. Route 9336 from Homestead southwest to Flamingo on Florida Bay allows us to trespass into a world of astonishing diversity, where some 300 species of birds, and twice that many types of fish, live or visit. Fourteen endangered species, including the Florida panther and the American crocodile, find haven in the Everglades, which itself is under enormous pressure from South Florida development. As the Everglades is all but perfectly flat—its flow is as shallow as six inches in spots, and its highest point of land is about 10 feet above sea level—Route 9336 can be taken in a breeze, but shouldn't be. Stop at the Royal Palm Visitor Center, the Pa-hay-okee Overlook, the Mahogany Hammock and West Lake; walk the boardwalks, and see alligators and eagles, saw-grass prairies and cypress swamps.

Eastern diamondback rattlesnake on a mangrove root in Florida Bay

Two Everglades stars:
the roseate spoonbill;
the American alligator

A Cuban tree frog

The Overseas Highway
Florida

In 1895 the Florida politician George W. Allen gave a speech out on Key West in which he envisioned "a highway across the Keys that should lead to every door in North America." At the time, when boats were the sole means of passage between the islands, he might as well have been predicting a rocket launch from Cape Canaveral to the moon. But once his notion was afloat, it proved irresistible, and, only a decade later, work began on what would become the Florida East Coast Railroad. Suddenly, mail, ice, other necessities—such as tourists—could be delivered to the Keys with ease, and a region populated only by farmers and fishermen was gradually transformed. The railroad was destroyed by a hurricane in 1935, and the next viable thoroughfare, the Overseas Highway, officially opened for traffic on July 4, 1938. Today, a drive from Florida City to Key West on the 127-mile, 42-bridge Route 1 is an oceangoing voyage unlike any other.

Seven Mile Bridge, Lower Keys

The end of the road: Key West

One boat at moor, another heading for sea from Marathon Key

Natchez Trace Parkway

Mississippi, Alabama, Tennessee

In this case, the highway is off the beaten path. The ancient Natchez Trace, the remnants of which the Parkway roughly parallels on a 444-mile journey from Natchez, Miss., up through Alabama to Nashville, is one of the world's oldest roads. It was cut, first, by buffalo and other migrating animals—"trace" derives from an old French word relating to footprints or animal tracks—then formalized by Native Americans, whose ancient burial mounds are still in rough evidence. Indian trade routes were later used by white traders and missionaries. There was, through the years, the presence of violence along the Trace, what with settlers, soldiers and highwaymen claiming it as their domain. The national parkway that received its initial authorization in 1934 still today insists upon a 40- or 50-mph speed limit, making for enjoyable driving. Better yet: Stroll some of the 63 miles of Natchez Trace National Scenic Trail in four separate areas along the Parkway, and listen to the echoes.

Above, Dunleith, Natchez; right, the original Trace, at mile 41.5 on the Parkway

Tim Fitzharris

Old Spanish Trail

Louisiana

Pinpointing the Old Spanish Trail can become confusing, as there are OST's everywhere across the South, including the famous one from Santa Fe to Los Angeles. Most of the other "Old Spanish Trail" fragments are frauds. Before there was a numbered U.S. Highway system, private companies built and marketed their own transcontinental roads based on themes. A particularly effective effort, which opened for travel in 1929, was the Old Spanish Trail. It was, from the first, based on a myth; the conquistadors never had a thoroughfare across the bottom of the country, though they traded and built forts in most areas. Today, US 90 mirrors or incorporates much of the 1929 Trail, and the section we recommend involves a 100-mile drive from Lafayette southeast to Houma in Louisiana on 90 and 182. The atmosphere is decidedly Cajun, with mossy trees shading the nation's largest river-overflow swamp and with the smell of gumbo thick in the air at each village along the way. A high point is the misty, moody basin of the Atchafalaya River in and around Morgan City.

Cypress grove, Lake Fausse Pointe

Fred Hirschmann

David Muench/Corbis

The massive trunks of bald cypresses in Atchafalaya Basin

Atchafalaya Basin at sunrise

The Lincoln Highway

It was, by the turn of the 19th century, a widely held dream: a cross-country road that would carry pioneers to the frontier. Congress set out to build such a thing in 1806; decades later, the road finally reached St. Louis, but it petered out there. Even into the 20th century, there was no cohesive route west, only a hodgepodge of mud roads maintained unevenly by the locals. But then, adventurers, bicyclists and automakers joined forces for the Good Roads Movement. They formed regional clubs boosting the routes they wanted paved, using dues for roadwork costs, signs and markers. The most successful group was the Lincoln Highway Association, which sought to build a road from New York to San Francisco. When the selected route was announced in 1913, several cities that were lucky enough to have been included declared a holiday. Excited Nebraskans celebrated with 300 miles of bonfires along their share of the highway, while Wyoming's governor declared there should be "an old-time jollification to include bonfires and general rejoicing." The glee was, of course, about the commercial opportunities to come. And for a time, the going was good indeed. A brief look at Bedford County, Pa., provides an example: In 1927 a restaurant in the shape of a coffeepot opened and couldn't brew java fast enough, while around the bend, in 1932, a sea-loving entrepreneur built the Ship Hotel into the side of the Alleghenies. Over the years, he drew in boarders from near and far with the boast that they could "see three states and seven counties" from his deck.

From top: Underwood Archives; Allan Grant

**Counterclockwise from left:
A Goodyear truck bears the words
BOSTON–SAN FRANCISCO VIA LINCOLN
HIGHWAY; a dappled Kearney, Neb.,
1948; that same year, Cheyenne, Wyo.;
the Coffee Pot building in 2003;
motorists in San Francisco stop at
The Stein for chow and beer in 1934.**

Calvin Coolidge slept there, as did Will Rogers, Thomas Edison and "Mr. Mobile," Henry Ford. Other idiosyncratic eateries and hostelries popped up along the highway and thrived for a while. But when ultramodern, transcontinental Route 80 opened in 1970, many of the quirky old outposts vanished. Before the Ship burned down in 2002, it had been closed for more than two decades. Today, sharp-eyed travelers can still see vestiges of the famous old road, as well as the occasional Lincoln Highway signpost, by heading out of New York City's Times Square through the Lincoln Tunnel, and pushing west on Route 30. As for the Lincoln Highway Association, it is now concerned with preservation rather than construction, and continually seeks artifacts from its beloved roadway for inclusion in its several museums along the highway. In 2003, preservationists helped save the Coffee Pot, which was moved off the main roadway to the Bedford County Fairgrounds, where it will be renovated.

Lake Michigan and Sleeping Bear Dunes National Lakeshore, Michigan

Jeff Gnass

North to the Lakes

David Muench

Red River Gorge Scenic Byway
Kentucky

Lexington and its environs are at the heart of Kentucky horse country, and certainly the equestrian facet of the region is lovely in its own right: Sweeping horse farms extending over the hillsides on either side of the country roads provide a luxurious setting that, one hopes, is somehow appreciated by the thoroughbreds. East of Lexington is a drive through the Daniel Boone National Forest that is quite different but no less splendid. For 46 miles from Stanton to Zachariah, through primeval woodland where ancient natives dwelled in caves, past tall waterfalls and alongside frothy streams, the Red River Gorge Scenic Byway is a rigorous Middle Earth to the horse country's sun-dappled meadows. Highlights of the drive include the river itself and over a hundred natural stone arches sculpted by 70 million years of erosion. In the Red River Gorge, with its spreading trees and cool waters, you truly have it made in the shade.

David Muench/Corbis

Sandstone Window Arch in Daniel Boone National Forest

Skyline Bridge in the Red River Gorge

A birch in the Red River Gorge Natural Preserve

Natural Bridge

David Muench

David Muench/Corbis

The Ohio River at Cave-in-Rock

Shawnee National Forest Drive

Illinois

In the southeastern part of the state, the "Illinois Ozarks"—the Shawnee Hills—rise above the mighty Ohio and Mississippi rivers. Surprising among highlands in the Midwest, they are strong and often dramatic; credit for this appends to merciful glaciers of the last ice age, which stopped 10 miles to the north, then retreated. A drive along Routes 34, Karbers Ridge Road, 1 and 146 from Mitchellsville in the north to New Liberty in the south is an exciting, 85-mile meander through Shawnee National Forest, where there are dense groves, impressive bluffs, serene streams and lakes. In the northern half of the journey, turn off 34 to Karbers Ridge, and do not miss two short detours that lead to vistas from High Knob and the aptly named Garden of the Gods. In the southern half along the Ohio, don't miss Cave-in-Rock State Park, where 18th century river pirates lay in wait to attack flatboats floating downriver.

Garden of the Gods

Covered Bridge Scenic Byway
Ohio

It is suitable that the covered bridge tour we include in this book is not set in Vermont or Iowa, for in the heyday of these rustic spans, Ohio had 2,000 of them—more than any other state. (Today, Indiana leads with 93 still standing; Ohio has 53.) The remnant bridges along southeastern Ohio's Scenic Byway, which runs north from Marietta along the Little Muskingum River, then through Wayne National Forest to Woodsfield, are fine specimens. A half mile off the Byway on Route 333 is Hills Covered Bridge, built in 1878, and farther upriver is Hune Covered Bridge, dating from 1879, and Knowlton Covered Bridge, built in 1887. Along the way you'll pass old red barns with MAIL POUCH TOBACCO signs painted on their sides, old oil rigs that still pump in dribs and drabs, old general stores—a cornucopia of old things. The 35-mile trip is a journey to a simpler time; it's all about tranquillity and grace, and if it is completed in less than two hours, then it has been hurried.

Farmland near Marietta

Above, Knowlton Covered
Bridge, Wayne National Forest;
right, the Hills/Hildred Covered
Bridge, Washington County;
opposite, Hune Covered Bridge
on the Little Muskingum River

The Amish Road
Indiana

I f there is a voyeuristic aspect to taking an auto tour through a community of people whose religion asks them to forgo cars (as well as other modern amenities including telephones and electricity), it is nonetheless true that this is a splendid way to drink in the quiet rhythms of life among the Amish. In fact, this is recommended at the Amish Country Visitors Center in Elkhart, where you can plunk down a deposit for the Heritage Trail Tour CD or cassette, a 90-minute tape that will assist you as you travel east on Routes 20, 13, 16, 250N and 200N. The history of the region and the Amish who began settling there in the 1840s is detailed, as are local attractions. And as you make your 28-mile trip through the village of Middlebury and past Amish farms that dot Crystal Valley between there and Shipshewana, drive very carefully: Just over the next hill may be a horse and buggy heading for market.

A buggy passing a barn in Shipshewana

Scenes on the farm: baling hay; cuddling a duckling

Route 22
Michigan

There are several interesting highways and byways along Great Lakes shores in the northern part of Michigan, but only 115.5-mile Route 22, between Traverse City and Manistee, passes by Sleeping Bear Dunes. You first head north from touristy Traverse City, which brags that its annual 100-million-pound harvest makes it the cherry capital of the world, to the top of the Leelanau Peninsula, then plunge southward along Lake Michigan's eastern shore. It is all orchards, fishing villages and vistas of the mighty lake as you travel from Northport through Leland and by Pyramid Point, Glen Arbor and Empire. Then comes Sleeping Bear Dunes National Lakeshore, a 71,176-acre sanctuary of sand and beach grass that is best sampled on the 7.4-mile Pierce Stocking Scenic Drive. Some of the dunes are nearly 500 feet high, among the world's tallest, and every moment spent in the park is a treasure. Don't finish there, though. Continue on past the Point Betsie Lighthouse to the pristine ports of Arcadia and Manistee, postcards come to life.

Swans at Sleeping Bear Dunes in winter

Point Betsie Lighthouse;
Cherry trees near Traverse City

The boardwalk at Sleeping Bear Dunes

The Great River Road

As long as people have been boating down rivers, we've been marking trails next to them—not least to provide a walking route home, when paddling upstream proved impossible. In the 1930s, Congress decided a parkway was needed along the Mississippi. By the time work started in the 1970s, the plan had been scaled back to improving and connecting all the little river roads into one long scenic byway on both sides of the river. So the Great River Road, which starts with the Mississippi in Lake Itasca, Minn., and travels through 10 states to the Gulf of Mexico, isn't really a single entity, and isn't scenic top to bottom. Certainly in some places it is: Even today you might round a bend and see paddleboats working the river—working it, these days, for the edification of the gamblers aboard. An astounding 15 percent

of U.S. freight still travels this Mississippi, and barges are ubiquitous. The Great River Road is some 3,000 miles long, about equivalent to a trip from New York to San Francisco, and thus, perhaps, beyond the limits of ordinary tourism. Those who do accept the challenge will be captivated as they watch the river wend its way southward. The upper Mississippi is so shallow, freighters need a navigational channel and 29 locks. The lower river is deep and meandering; the serpentine waterway is nearly three times as long as its valley. There are 300-foot bluffs in places, and elsewhere, stretches of farmland frame an awesome expanse of water. As it should, the Great River Road, carrying no specific number but marked by green ship-wheel signs, passes by Hannibal, Mo., birthplace of the river's patron saint, Mark Twain.

Alfred Eisenstaedt

Clockwise from left: A paddleboat plies its way along the Mighty Mississippi, 1950; the St. Louis Gateway Arch, here under construction, was completed in 1965; a blustery winter day in Illinois; a trestle bridge spans the river in Natchez, Miss.

Sweet clover, Custer State Scenic Drive, South Dakota

Through the Heartland

North Shore Scenic Drive

Minnesota

Split Rock Lighthouse and Lake Superior; opposite, palisades at Tettegouche State Park

Driving along the southeastern shore of Lake Superior in Wisconsin is by no means a second-tier experience, as the constant interplay of the great North Woods and the world's largest freshwater lake makes for rapturous music. But just across the state line in Duluth, a northbound shoreline drive begins what will build to an even more affecting coda. Upon leaving the city, impressions of upcountry wilderness are instant as you cross at least five rivers and thrill to that many more dramatic lake views before reaching Two Harbors, barely 22 miles up the road. From here to trail's end at Grand Portage on the Canadian border is 132 miles of unadulterated and increasingly commanding scenery: the ever denser Superior National Forest on your left, the craggy shore and a mosaic of whitecaps on your right, a diminishing number of quaint villages, then . . . nothing . . . the wind . . . a wolf's howl.

Grand Portage Indian Reservation: a timber wolf; Holy Rosary Catholic Church; wood lilies and shrubby cinquefoil

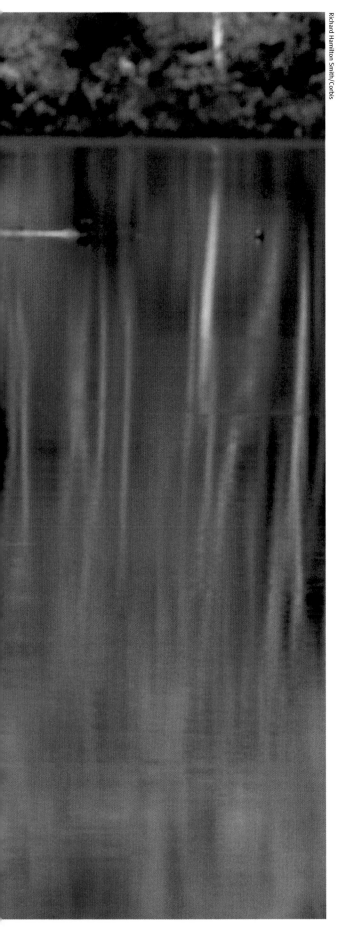

Richard Hamilton Smith/Corbis

Phil Schermeister/Corbis

Edge of the Wilderness Scenic Byway

Minnesota

If this road, also identifiable as Route 38 from Effie south to Grand Rapids, is supposedly skirting the edge of the wilderness, then where is the center? The main part of this two-lane thoroughfare in north-central Minnesota moves through dense Chippewa National Forest, and a visitor should be on the lookout not only for birds such as bald eagles (the nation's largest population) and wild turkeys, and mammals such as coyotes and raccoons, but also moose, wolves and bears. A not-to-be-missed shunpike off the Byway is a 17.5-mile loop called the Chippewa Adventure, which begins in Marcell, about halfway down 47-mile-long Route 38. Shut off the engine for a bit and listen for the loons that call Minnesota's many lakes home. And in autumn, the Edge of the Wilderness is the equal of New Hampshire's Kancamagus or Vermont's Route 100.

Chippewa National Forest

Peter Norbeck and Custer Scenic Byways

South Dakota

A trip along these two byways plus an extra 18 miles on the Custer State Park Wildlife Loop Road make for more than 100 miles of touring through the Black Hills of South Dakota. There is astonishing diversity of topography as you climb from prairie floor up and over rough mountains, alternately calmed by views of serene lakes and left awestruck by the "needles"—large and jagged pillars of granite. The chief attraction in the area, which can be seen from various vantages but is best experienced from three miles distant on the Norbeck Memorial Overlook, is man-made: the 60-foot sculpture on Mount Rushmore. By the way, we know who Custer was, but Peter Norbeck? He was the South Dakota politician who, back in the 1920s, pushed for the road now named after him, and once said of the area: "You're not supposed to drive here at 60 miles an hour. To do the scenery half justice, people should drive 20 or under. To do it full justice, they should get out and walk."

Bison in Custer State Park; baby bison

In the Black Hills: top, Needles Eye; Mount Rushmore;
right, Black Elk Wilderness

Fred Hirschmann

North Unit Scenic Drive
North Dakota

Bill Clinton and Dwight Eisenhower had their golf, Jack Kennedy had his touch football and Harry Truman had his daily constitutionals, but Teddy Roosevelt claimed the whole outdoors—to hunt in, ride horses in, generally revel in. He was by far the greatest naturalist among our Presidents, and for his accomplishments in protecting public lands, boosting the National Park Service and establishing the National Forest Service, he will forever remain the greatest. It is altogether fitting that a 70,447-acre part of North Dakota that he knew well and loved dearly—he returned to the state soon after his wife's death—is now sanctified as the Theodore Roosevelt National Park. Within it is a 14-mile drive from the visitors' center to Oxbow Overlook that is a living evocation of TR's rough-and-ready, tough-but-gentle spirit. You are traveling through what are known as badlands, but consider the ocher rocks and the straw-brown valley floor, the longhorns and bison grazing as they did when Teddy rode the range. There is a solemn, western, cowboy poetry at play on this short drive.

Badlands, Theodore Roosevelt National Park

Grazing bison

The Little Missouri River

Arkansas Scenic 7 Byway

Arkansas

The government agencies that hand out the designations have put a lot of pressure on this stretch of two-lane blacktop extending from Harrison down to Hot Springs. The U.S. Forest Service has honored the 60.6 miles of 7 that pass through the Ozark and Ouachita national forests as a National Forest Scenic Byway. The winding and often steep roadway runs over hills and mountains, through forests and valleys, affording endless scenes of natural splendor. Right near the start, you cross the Buffalo National River and Arkansas's own Grand Canyon, from which the Boston Mountains can be viewed. Midway to Hot Springs, take a side trip into a remote part of the Ozark National Forest on a twisty, challenging loop drive that begins at Dardanelle— and which is every bit as scenic as Scenic 7.

Sunrise in Ozark National Forest

Beaver Jim Villines cabin, along the Buffalo National River

Route 66

For all its swingin' image—"get your kicks on Route Sixty-six"—U.S. Highway 66 is better understood under its homey nicknames, the Main Street of America and the Mother Road. It was, from the first, designed to link previously isolated small towns in the Heartland and the Southwest so that farmers could transport produce for redistribution. In 1926, the year after Congress passed the comprehensive version of its Highways Act, the number "66" was assigned to an idea that had been promulgated by two entrepreneurs, Cyrus Avery of Tulsa and John Woodruff of Springfield, Mo. They didn't envision a road merely to get people from here to there—east-west or north-south—but, rather, a diagonal from Chicago to Los Angeles that would be about shipping, and about stitching the West together. During the Depression, unemployed men worked to make the highway "continuously paved," still a novelty for a long road

Bettmann/Corbis

Andreas Feininger

when 2,400-mile Route 66 was finished in 1938. An army of the poor tried to flee the Dust Bowl on the new highway, as John Steinbeck recounted in *The Grapes of Wrath:* "They come into 66 from the tributary side roads, from the wagon tracks and the rutted country roads, 66 is the mother road, the road of flight." Among the throng who migrated west on 66 in the postwar era was a pianist from Pennsylvania, Robert William Troup Jr., who penned his famous anthem in 1946 immediately after landing in L.A. Nat King Cole's version of Bobby Troup's song was a smash that year, and, in the decades since, Chuck Berry, the Rolling Stones and several generations of Americans have gotten a kick from "Route 66." Although the road has been decommissioned and diced into 44 state roads, nostalgia dies hard, and HISTORIC ROUTE 66 signs still mark most of the passage. Travelers can still find their way to the Wigwam Motel in Arizona, the Zia Motor Lodge in Albuquerque or the Cozy Dog Drive-In in Illinois—just as earlier pilgrims of Route 66 did, back when the road was Mother.

Counterclockwise from above: In 1945, one week before the end of World War II, a car and trailer traverse the California desert; two years later, Andreas Feininger took this famous photograph in Seligman, Ariz.; the Boots Motel, built in Carthage, Mo., in 1939, played host to Clark Gable and Gene Autry; a 1992 view of Cadillac Ranch in Amarillo, Tex.; a terribly tacky tableau on Los Angeles' Sunset Boulevard.

Red Mountain Pass, San Juan Mountains, Colorado

Over the Mountains

Laurence Parent

Billy the Kid Trail
New Mexico

It is to be supposed that such as Billy the Kid, Pat Garrett and "Black Jack" Pershing—along with another local denizen, Smokey the Bear—once took the scenery in Lincoln County for granted. But several current agencies dedicated to drawing attention to the finest auto routes have clearly taken notice, as evidenced by the fact that the so-called Billy the Kid Trail, 84 miles of highway in the heart of the Old West, is not only a National Scenic Byway but a State Scenic Byway, to boot. The Trail is a loop composed of U.S. Routes 70 and 380 and New Mexico's Route 48, with additional attractions on a cutacross, New Mexico 220. In contrast with the desert that surrounds it, this mountainous region is green and cool wherever it isn't rocky. The echoes of gunfire ring through each mile as the rugged horizon transports you to the 19th century, when desperadoes rode the range with lawmen hot on their trail.

**Late day at the base of
the Sacramento Mountains**

Trail Ridge Road
Colorado

Mountain scenes which stir one's blood and which strengthen and sweeten life," declared naturalist Enos Mills of the extraordinary realm of the high Rockies, 416 square miles of which, in 1915, became Rocky Mountain National Park. Five years later, Old Fall River Road opened for high-country auto tours, but the single-lane, super-steep (grades of 15 percent!) track soon proved unacceptable. Trail Ridge Road, so named since it followed the migratory path of ancient natives across the Rockies, was built as a replacement by 1932, and its 44 miles of two-lane travel still form America's highest continuously paved road. Heading west from Deer Ridge Junction, the highway climbs almost 4,000 feet very quickly, then spends 11 miles above 11,000 feet in altitude, four miles above 12,000 feet—cresting at 12,183 feet between Lava Cliffs and Gore Range. The road is closed by snow from mid-October till Memorial Day each year, but in midsummer, with the wildflowers abloom, it may be the summit of driving experiences.

Yellow-bellied marmot; Rocky Mountain bighorn

A Trail Ridge tarn; snowy aspens

Carr Clifton/Minden Pictures

San Juan Skyway
Colorado

Whereas the Trail Ridge Road is something of a hair-raising, lung-busting sprint across the Continental Divide on the roof of America, the San Juan Skyway is a hither-and-yon tour of Colorado's mountainous southwest—a 232-mile route best enjoyed over more than one day. A loop beginning and ending in Durango (or Silverton, or Ridgeway, or Telluride, or wherever else you choose), the Skyway rides through parts of two national forests, and up and over the San Juan Mountains. It also touches upon Mesa Verde National Park, a site not to be missed. Here in the Montezuma Valley are the 2,000-foot-high cliffside dwellings built between the 6th and 13th centuries by the Anasazi, ancestors of the Pueblo Indians who, after their golden age, mysteriously disappeared. Today, jazz fills the air at summertime festivals in the region, while in winter the schuss and boom of world-class skiing is heard in Telluride and the ominously named Purgatory.

Aspens and conifers,
Uncompahgre National Forest

Larry Ulrich

Sneffels Range, San Juan Mountains

Balcony House, Mesa Verde National Park

Kaibab Plateau– North Rim Parkway

Arizona

There can be little arguing that the ultimate way to take in the Grand Canyon is by raft or kayak, floating the waters of the Colorado River, which after six million years is still busily at work, cleaving into bedrock, continuing to carve a gorge that is already a mile deep. But so grand is the Grand that there are pleasures aplenty to be had at ground level (which is to say, above the rim). The 44-mile Scenic Parkway that leads from the community of Jacob Lake to the edge of the North Rim, which is 1,000 feet higher than the South, travels across a high-elevation plateau, through the dense aspen and ponderosa pine woodlands of Kaibab National Forest, delivering you with a flourish to one of this world's truly awesome vistas. You must get out of your car to confront this natural wonder, an experience not to be missed in one's lifetime.

Greenland Lake on the Kaibab Plateau

Larry Ulrich

Tim Fitzharris

Grand Canyon National Park: Left, rock
formations overlooking the Colorado River;
above, Mount Hayden from the North Rim

Carr Clifton/Minden Pictures

Tim Fitzharris

Snowy Range Road
Wyoming

As the nickname for the 85-mile drive along Wyoming Route 130 implies, you can taste a little bit of winter even during summer in the Medicine Bow Mountains. (And you can't touch this road in real winter, as it is snowed under.) When you drive west from Laramie toward the mountain range, the flatland traveling is easy. After you've passed through the town of Centennial, it becomes intriguing: You enter a forest of aspen and lodgepole pine, with ponds and meadows adding grace notes. (Watch here for moose and elk.) Soon you are above the timberline, and the Snowy Range appears majestically before you. The road travels higher still, past glaciated lakes to the pass at Libby Flats (10,847 feet), from which you can see, on a clear day, all the way to the Colorado Rockies. The drive down to the North Platte River, thence to Saratoga, caps an exhilarating sojourn amidst the summits.

The Diamond, Medicine Bow Mountains

Tim Fitzharris

Larry Ulrich

**Left, Medicine Bow Mountains at Snowy Range Pass;
above, alpine phlox**

Beartooth Highway

Montana, Wyoming

With the possible exception of Jack Kerouac, no American of the 20th century was more noted for going on the road than commentator Charles Kuralt, and it was his considered opinion that the Beartooth is, simply, "America's most beautiful road." The 68-mile stretch of Route 212 beginning in Red Lodge, Mont., and ending in Cooke City, Mont., at the northeastern entrance to Yellowstone National Park—having along the way dipped into Wyoming's Shoshone National Forest—was designated a National Scenic Byway in 1989. It is that in spades, as becomes evident after the quick ascent from Red Lodge onto the enormous Beartooth Plateau, at 3,000 square miles one of North America's largest land masses above 10,000 feet. There are hundreds of alpine lakes and unequaled mountain views on the drive, and there's history as well. In 1882, Civil War legend Gen. Philip Sheridan, with the aid of a local hunter, led the first successful crossing of the Beartooth Mountains along the very route that, in 1936, would become Beartooth Highway.

Beartooth Mountains, Shoshone National Forest

Beartooth Mountains; above, Long Lake, Shoshone National Forest

Centennial Scenic Byway
Wyoming

There is very little driving in and around Yellowstone and Grand Teton national parks that is not scenic in the extreme; none other than Theodore Roosevelt, as formidable an outdoorsman as he was a statesman, felt that the "valley drive" east from Yellowstone to Cody was the country's finest roadway. While we have no quarrel with TR's choice, we would suggest that picking that stretch through bear country rather than any of the three drives in Teton, or the many drives in phantasmagorical Yellowstone, is only an invitation to debate. We nominate the Wyoming Centennial Scenic Byway, a 162-mile horseshoe that extends through the Shoshone and Bridger-Teton national forests from Dubois to Moran Junction and down to Pinedale, only because it affords maximum bang for the buck. The Green River Valley, the Teton Range, Jackson Hole, the Wind River Range, the National Elk Refuge, the Snake River: They are all here, on one of the country's most spellbinding routes.

Badger

Grand Teton National Park

A gang of male elk in the National Elk Refuge

David Muench

Galen Rowell/Mountain Light

Going-to-the-Sun Road

Montana

Glacier National Park was already known as the Crown of the Continent when, in 1918, National Park Service Chief Engineer George Goodwin proposed a road through it, one that would climb up to and over Logan Pass on the Continental Divide. The resultant 50-mile byway, a quarter of its length carved out of mountainside, didn't open until 1933, after years of painstaking preparation and backbreaking work. Since this was a park road, all care was taken to yield the best scenery—it travels the length of Lake McDonald before heading for the pass, then the length of St. Mary Lake on its way down—while preserving landscape. The name of the road, by the way, comes not from its impressive grade, but from nearby Going-to-the-Sun Mountain. It is nonetheless suitable, as former park superintendent J. Ross Eakin averred in 1933: "It gives the impression that in driving this road autoists will ascend to extreme heights and view sublime panoramas."

Wildflowers near Logan Pass; St. Mary Lake

A mountain goat at Logan Pass

Beargrass, Logan Pass

Highway 12
Utah

Much that is along this 124-mile, east-west route across south-central Utah is impressive: 11,000-foot high Boulder Mountain, the Escalante Petrified Forest, two wondrous small canyons named Tropic and Red, the miracle of Dixie National Forest rising in the highlands above the Utah desert. But one place makes the word "impressive" seem small: Bryce Canyon National Park, through which Highway 12 proceeds. "Red rocks standing like men in a bowl-shaped canyon," was how the native Paiute Indians described the fantastical stone formations that fill Bryce Amphitheater. When the state's citizenry promoted the area as a park for federal protection in 1919, they called it the Temple of the Gods. More prosaically, the natural statuary is known as a collection of hoodoos—hooded spectres haunting the canyon. By whatever name, these singular, signature features of Bryce Canyon never fail to elicit awe.

**Bryce hoodoos: Thor's Hammer, above;
view from Inspiration Point**

Fred Hirschmann

Larry Ulrich

Markagunt Plateau in Dixie National Forest

Bristle cone pines, Bryce Canyon National Park

Scott T. Smith/Larry Ulrich Stock

Jeff Gnass

Lake Tahoe—Eastshore Drive

Nevada

In the rugged and often dusty West there is a drive that competes with the roads hugging the Great Lakes for designation as the country's loveliest, most dramatic freshwater itinerary. This is the 28-mile Eastshore Drive at Lake Tahoe, running from Stateline, Nev., in the south to the northeast point of the lake. As you head out on Highway 50, the road is winding, and views open repeatedly to the pristine alpine lake surrounded by the snowcapped Sierra Nevada Mountains. A distinctive change of scenery occurs after you've passed through the tunnel at Cave Rock and continue east on Route 50 along the old Pony Express route that bisects the Great Basin—known, east of Carson City, as the Loneliest Road in America. But to further savor the shimmering lake, whose crystal clear water exceeds 1,600 feet deep in places, proceed north on State Route 28 to Incline Village. The entire Rim of the Lake drive is 72 miles long, but views from the western side can't compare to those from the eastern.

Lake Tahoe Nevada State Park

Bettmann/Corbis

The Las Vegas Strip

On 74 of the country's 75 official Scenic Byways, as designated by the Federal Highway Administration, you miss out on much of the natural splendor if you travel after dark. But the unnatural wonders of the 96th sanctioned Byway, the Las Vegas Strip, make it much better at night. The Strip has more than 5,000 miles of neon tubing for each of its three miles. With the Bellagio Hotel & Casino's 240-foot-high waterspouts aglow in spotlights and a 315,000-watt beam shooting forth from the crown of the 30-story Luxor Resort, gambling's mecca is brighter from outer space than New York City, Los Angeles or Tokyo. Vegas's transformation has been so thorough that it's hard to imagine that in 1931, when gambling was first legalized there, it was a one-hotel oasis in the desert. What became the town's—and then the city's—main thoroughfare has had several names: Route 91, Los Angeles Highway, Fifth Street. But it was "the Las Vegas Strip" that stuck. (As is fitting, the descriptive nickname was the notion of a vice squad captain, Guy McAfee of L.A., who was inspired by his hometown's Sunset Strip.) This Scenic Byway differs from all the others in this volume and on the Highway Administration's list in still another way: There is perhaps no other road in America that has so many people closely associated with it. When you think "Las Vegas Strip," you don't think about blacktop; you think Sinatra, Dino, Sammy, Liberace, Gleason, Elvis, Barbra and today: Wayne Newton, Celine Dion, Siegfried & Roy . . .

Counterclockwise from far left: The turning point was 1931—gambling was legalized, work began on the Hoover Dam, and divorce laws were liberalized. Here, three years later, things are just beginning to pick up; in the '40s, Meyer Lansky watches over the construction of The Flamingo, his brainchild with Bugsy Siegel, and the first of the lavish casinos; nothing else on earth can match the spectacular glitz that is Vegas.

Route 1 along the Pacific coast at Big Sur, California

The Pacific Coast— And Beyond

Mount Baker Scenic Byway

Washington

If dizzying heights unsettle you, this drive, a 24-mile section of Highway 542 east of Glacier, may best be shunned. But if you're game, this adventure will yield the kind of views usually reserved for high-country hikers. The first piece of the drive is anything but harrowing, as you wind through an old-growth evergreen forest, with the North Fork Nooksack River rushing alongside. After seven miles, head down Wells Creek Road for less than a mile; there you will see Nooksack Falls tumbling and crashing over a 175-foot rock ledge—one of many waterfalls responsible for the Cascade Mountains' name. From the falls, the Byway travels another relatively straightforward half dozen miles, then morphs into a switchback mountain road that, over 10 miles, climbs 3,200 feet in altitude. Near trail's end are Heather Meadows and Picture Lake, with wondrous views of 9,127-foot Mount Shuksan. Your rewards keep coming: At Artist Point, accessible in summer, there's a close-up view of grand Mount Baker itself, made all the more intriguing by the fact that it's an active volcano.

Mount Shuksan and Picture Lake

Moss-covered big leaf maples in the Hoh Rain Forest

The Olympic Peninsula
Washington

The diversity of topography and flora on display in the northwestern corner of the country is such that we cannot recommend a single byway, but must cite four. First is the biggie, Route 101, a loop from Aberdeen Harbor on the Pacific coast up and around Olympic National Park and Forest, then back down along the Hood Canal to Olympia—nearly 300 miles in all, some of it splendid with views of the ocean, some of it weirdly fun in a *Twin Peaks* way, and some of it . . . well, dreary. At least twice, depart 101 and head into the Park: on the Hoh River Road that takes you to an extraordinary rain forest, and on Hurricane Ridge Road, which for 17 miles hosts vantages of the Olympic Mountains to the south and the Cascades, distant in the north. A third shunpike off 101 is the Strait of Juan de Fuca Highway, a 61-mile stretch along the shore of a glacial fjord connecting Puget Sound and the Pacific. In one strange place, so many worlds.

Ruby Beach, western coast of the Olympic Peninsula

Wild columbine

**Unicorn Peak and Unicorn Horn
from Hurricane Ridge Road**

Cascade Lakes Scenic Byway
Oregon

I t's always sunny along the 66 miles of Routes 372 and 46 from Bend down to Crescent and Odell lakes. Well, perhaps not always—but an average of nearly 300 days a year are sunny in central Oregon, since the Cascade Mountains just to the west form an effective barrier against wet air from the Pacific. The sunshine serves to add glitter to a region already resplendent in natural beauty, as it reflects off distant glaciers and dozens of near-at-hand lakes and ponds. From Bend, Route 372 climbs into the Deschutes National Forest and then past the 9,065-foot, conical Mt. Bachelor, a world-class ski area and a summit from which tourists can see to California and Washington. As you drive on and then turn south on Route 46, the lakes arrive in profusion: Sparks and Devils and Elk and Hosmer and Lava and Little Lava and Cultus and Crane Prairie (actually, a reservoir) and Davis . . . It's a land o' lakes—and sunlight.

Left, Broken Top and Sparks Lake; above, Proxy Falls in Deschutes National Forest

Rogue-Umpqua Scenic Byway
Oregon

The same Cascade Range that keeps central Oregon sunny and dry by intercepting Pacific Ocean moisture is, as you might expect, rather wet on its western slopes. This is not necessarily a bad thing, as towering waterfalls and frothing rivers only add to the character of a region that is already thunderously dramatic with signs of ancient volcanic action. The 172-mile Byway describes a sideways U from one I-5 town (Roseburg) to another (Gold Hill), and spends much of its time in the dense Umpqua National Forest. Three attractions not to be missed: Colliding Rivers Viewpoint, where the North Umpqua and Little rivers crash head-on into each other; Watson Falls, at 272 feet the highest in southern Oregon, and star of the "Highway of Waterfalls"; and Crater Lake National Park, a short side trip off the Byway to a clear blue lake sitting placidly in the mouth of a volcano that last blew 6,800 years ago.

Above, Watson Falls; right, Crater Lake

Mesquite Flat Sand Dunes

Death Valley Scenic Byway

California

And now for something completely different: a trip to the hottest, driest, lowest place in the United States. Sound charming? Well, it is, in its unique way. The 81.5-mile Scenic Byway, a section of Route 190 that is entirely within the boundaries of 3.3-million-acre Death Valley National Park, travels down from the Panamint Mountains into the valley, past Stovepipe Wells Village and then miles of sand dunes, across the flats of Devils Cornfield to the Salt Creek Nature Trail. Nurtured by underground springs, this oasis can be toured by foot on a boardwalk loop. Then it's back in the car and on to Furnace Creek and, ultimately, a climb to Zabriskie Point, a 710-foot overlook from which the whole undisturbed, complex ecosystem can be viewed. In the distance are mountains, lava flows and a world of sand; out there are mesquite and cactus, rattlesnakes and owls and bobcats. And precious little else.

Salt marsh and the Panamint Range

Carr Clifton/Minden Pictures (2)

Michael Melford

Tim Fitzharris

Desert prickly pear cactus

Giant dunes east of Stovepipe Wells Village

Tim Fitzharris

Route 1

California

Many scenic highways have one standout aspect that informs their personalities, be it this mountain or prairie or ocean view. Route 1, which runs down the Pacific coast of California for 672 miles, has it all. A good place to begin is Pacifica, just below San Francisco. Two eye-filling hours later you enter historic Monterey, formerly home to Steinbeck's Cannery Row and now known for its sensational aquarium. The nonstop sensory gratification continues as you drive along Ocean View Boulevard and especially 17-Mile Drive, a pay-per-view tour of the headlands that may be America's premier side road. After the charm of Carmel-by-the-Sea comes the sturm und drang of Point Lobos and, then, the awesome Big Sur. As you cross Bixby Bridge, 260 feet above crashing ocean waves, you are aloft in your car. And Route 1 never quits: The Los Padres National Forest rises up to your left, then yields to the Santa Lucia Mountains. In Morro Bay there are seaside dunes and inland pastures aplenty. Route 1 is the Golden State's 24-karat drive.

The Big Sur coast

The Lone Cypress, on rock outcropping, 17-Mile Drive

Northern elephant seals at Point Piedras Blanca

Tim Fitzharris

Herald Sund

**Above, Portage
Glacier; opposite,
an aurora above the
Chugach Mountains**

The Seward Highway
Alaska

I n the past, this 127-mile route from Anchorage around the Turnagain Arm
inlet, then south across the Kenai Peninsula, was used by migrating native
Alaskans, Russian explorers, gold miners, fur trappers, Iditarod Trail pioneers
and their sled dogs, and rail passengers. By 1951 the various links of a road system had been pieced together, and within a few years, the highway was paved.
Although Alaska is vast, diverse and complex, in this single drive you can par-
take of many of the state's otherworldly glories. The cold chop of Turnagain Arm
(so named when Captain Cook had to turn away at this point in his frustrated
quest for the Northwest Passage); the glaciers; the rugged mountains and high
meadows of the peninsula, decorated with wildflowers and waterfalls; the eagles,
moose and Dall sheep; the blue water of Kenai Lake; the fjords off Seward in
Resurrection Bay: This is the Oz that is Alaska. The Seward Highway is one of
21 America's Byways that have been designated by the Secretary of Trans-
portation as an All-American Road, "Best of the Best."

Kenai Lake; a mountain goat above Exit Glacier

David Muench

Hana Highway
Hawaii

This narrow, winding, 53-mile route along the northeastern shore of Maui is not for the faint of heart, or the heavy of foot. With dozens of one-lane bridges, hundreds of hairpin turns and blind curves, and speed limits in many places of 15 mph (and that's one liberal law), the road from Kahului to Hana on Routes 36 and 360 is difficult, even treacherous in places. But taken at a sane pace, its rewards are bountiful. As you zigzag up, down and all around the slopes near Twin Falls, it is easy to see that Hana Highway started life as a footpath. There are waterfalls only slightly inland, and then you're back out by the shore, where sea spray shoots up over lava outcroppings. At trail's end you turn the car around, take a deep breath, and return via the same road—the only one available in this exotic part of paradise.

Jean Miele/Corbis

Above, the winding road; right, lava outcroppings

Mindanao gum trees in the Keanae Arboretum

Seven Sacred Pools at Oheo Gulch

Just One More

Robert Lackenbach

Slow Down! Enjoy the View!

This driver at the fifth annual Pebble Beach, Calif., sports-car rally, in 1954,

is taking the enchanting 17-Mile Drive at much too quick a pace.